T0395143

NOISY ANIMALS

Say "How Are You?"

on the Farm

By Madeline Tyler

maple bay

www.littlebluehousebooks.com

Copyright © 2025 by Little Blue House, Mendota Heights, MN 55120. All rights reserved. No part of this book may be reproduced or utilized in any form or by any means without written permission from the publisher.

Little Blue House is distributed by North Star Editions: sales@northstareditions.com | 888-417-0195

Library of Congress Control Number: 2024936702

ISBN
979-8-89359-009-8 (hardcover)
979-8-89359-019-7 (paperback)
979-8-89359-039-5 (ebook pdf)
979-8-89359-029-6 (hosted ebook)

Printed in the United States of America
Mankato, MN
082024

Written by: Madeline Tyler

Edited by: Robin Twiddy

Designed by: Jasmine Pointer

QR by: Kelby Twyman

All facts, statistics, web addresses and URLs in this book were verified as valid and accurate at time of writing. No responsibility for any changes to external websites or references can be accepted by either the author or publisher.

Image & Sound credits
All images courtesy of Shutterstock.com. With thanks to Getting Images, Thinkstock Photo, and iStockphoto.

All sounds (s) by http://soundbible.com. Character – Lorelyn Medina . Front Cover – Vectors Bang. 3 – Johnny Adolphson. 3 – vishwesh trivedi. 4 – stephan (s). 5 – vishwesh trivedi. 6 – Bachkova Natalia, Mike Koenig (s). 7 – StockSmartStart. 8 – dezy, Mike Koenig (s). 9 – Hanaha, Mintoboru. 10 – Mimadeo. 11 – Mintoboru. 12 – Edward Westmacott, fws.gov (s). 13 – Maquiladora. 14 – J R Patterson, BuffBill84 (s). 15 – curiosity. 16 – Dora Zett. 17 – Gaidamashchuk, Hanaha. 18 – Tory Kallman, bod (s). 19 – bilha golan, Mintoboru. 20 – Dmitry Kalinovsky, Caroline Ford (s). 21 – Mintoboru. 22 – makspogonii, BlastwaveFx.com (s). 23 – Mintoboru, Valeri Hadeev.

To use the QR codes in this book, a grown-up will need to set one of these apps as the default browser on the device you are using:

. Chrome
. Safari
. Firefox
. Ecosia

Your QR app might open the links in this book right away. If it doesn't, tap the button that says "open," "continue," "browse," or something similar.

Lots of animals live on the farm. It can get very noisy!

Scan the QR code to hear the noises of the farm.

4

Roosters crow in the morning and tell all the other animals that it is the start of a new day.

Say "how are you?" and then scan the QR code.

6

Cock-a-doodle-doooo!

7

Horses like to eat grass, hay, oats, and barley.

Say "how are you?" and then scan the QR code.

8

Neigh!

9

A group of sheep is called a flock.

10

Baaaaaaaa!

11

Geese like to live in grassy areas near water.

Say "how are you?" and then scan the QR code.

12

Honk, honk, honk!

13

Most of the milk that you can buy comes from dairy cows that live on farms.

Say "how are you?" and then scan the QR code.

14

Moooo!

Rabbits have long ears
and fluffy tails.

How are you?

Can you reply like a rabbit?

16

Sniff sniff, nibble nibble!

17

This turkey has a big tail
made up of lots of feathers.

Say "how are you?"
and then scan
the QR code.

18

Gobble, gobble, gobble!

This pig has a snout that it uses
to find food in the ground.

Say "how are you?"
and then scan
the QR code.

20

Oink!

Baby goats are called kids.

Say "how are you?" and then scan the QR code.

22

Mehhhheheheh!

23

24